the Greatest Gift

Rebecca Germany

The greatest gift was. . . ?

A baby?

And is it true?

And is it true,

This most tremendous tale of all,

Seen in a stained-glass window's hue,

A Baby in an ox's stall?

The Maker of the stars and sea

Became a Child on earth for me?

Sir John Betjeman

Gold,
incense,
and
myrrh?

The magi, as you know, were wise men—
wonderfully wise men who brought gifts
to the Babe in the manger.
They invented the art of giving
Christmas presents.

O. HENRY

❖   ❖   ❖

On coming to the house, they saw the child
with his mother Mary,
and they bowed down and worshiped him.
Then they opened their treasures and presented him
with gifts of gold and of incense and of myrrh.

MATTHEW 2:11

A
wonderful
holiday?

It's Christmastime!

It's Christmastime!

I'm so happy it's Christmastime!

Hearts are happy and songs are gay

God's Son was born on Christmas Day.

Wanda Royer

Peace on earth will come to stay,

When we live Christmas

every day.

Helen Steiner Rice

The
Greatest
Gift Is
Love!

Love was born Yesterday

Love lives Today

Love reigns Forever

When we celebrate Christmas
we are celebrating that amazing time
when the Word that shouted all
the galaxies into being,
limited all power,
and for love of us came to us
in the powerless body
of a human baby.

MADELEINE L'ENGLE

Yesterday

For God so loved the world
that he gave his one and only Son,
that whoever believes in him
shall not perish but have eternal life.

JOHN 3:16

Love came down at Christmas,
Love all lovely, Love Divine;
Love was born at Christmas;
Star and angels gave the sign.

CHRISTINA ROSSETTI

❖   ❖   ❖

Good news from heaven the angels bring,
Glad tidings to the earth they sing:
To us this day a child is given,
To crown us with the joy of heaven.

MARTIN LUTHER

He is the image of the invisible God,

the firstborn over all creation.

COLOSSIANS 1:15

Jesus did not come

to make God's love possible,

but to make God's love visible.

AUTHOR UNKNOWN

Christ was not half a God and half a man;
he was perfectly God and perfectly man.

JAMES STALKER

◆　　◆　　◆

On Christmas Day
two thousand years ago,
the birth of a tiny baby in an
obscure village in the Middle East
was God's supreme triumph of good over evil.

CHARLES COLSON

More light than we can learn,

More wealth than we can treasure,

More love than we can earn,

More peace than we can measure,

Because one Child is born.

AUTHOR UNKNOWN

◆　　◆　　◆

Love's mark on history. . .

All history is incomprehensible without Christ.

ERNEST RENAN

The birth of the baby Jesus
stands as the most significant
event in all history,
because it has meant the pouring into
a sick world of the healing medicine of love
which has transformed all manner of hearts
for almost two thousand years. . . .

GEORGE MATTHEW ADAMS

◆   ◆   ◆

As the centuries pass the evidence
is accumulating that,
measured by His effect on history,
Jesus is the most influential life
ever lived on this planet.

KENNETH SCOTT LATOURETTE

Jesus Christ will still be important for mankind
two or three thousand years hence.

H. G. WELLS

◆　　　◆　　　◆

A Cross Built by Love

The Christmas message is that there is

hope for a ruined humanity—

hope of pardon,

hope of peace with God,

hope of glory—

because at the Father's will Jesus Christ became poor,

and was born in a stable so that thirty years later

He might hang on a cross.

J. I. PACKER

Nails could not have kept Jesus on the cross
had love not held Him there.

AUTHOR UNKNOWN

◆　　　◆　　　◆

He came to pay a debt he did not owe,
because we owed a debt we could not pay.

AUTHOR UNKNOWN

◆　　　◆　　　◆

Christ's blood is heaven's key.

THOMAS BROOKS

Jesus Christ's claim of divinity is
the most serious claim anyone ever made.
Everything about Christianity hinges on
His incarnation, crucifixion, and resurrection.
That's what Christmas, Good Friday,
and Easter are all about.

LUIS PALAU

God proved his love on the cross.
When Christ hung, and bled, and died,
it was God saying to the world—I love you.

BILLY GRAHAM

Today

What can I give him,

Poor as I am?

If I were a shepherd,

I would bring a lamb,

If I were a Wise Man,

I would do my part—

Yet what I can, I give Him,

Give my heart.

CHRISTINA ROSSETTI

Salvation is found in no one else,

for there is no other name under heaven given to men

by which we must be saved.

ACTS 4:12

❖   ❖   ❖

The Early Christians believed that salvation is

a gift from God but that God gives his gift to

whomever he chooses. And he chooses to give

it to those who love and obey him.

D. W. BERCOT

❖   ❖   ❖

For it is by grace you have been saved, through faith—

and this not from yourselves, it is the gift of God.

EPHESIANS 2:8

This day and your life are God's gifts to you:
so give thanks and be joyful always!

JIM BEGGS

◆　　◆　　◆

Every good and perfect gift is from above, coming
down from the Father of the heavenly lights, who does
not change like shifting shadows.

JAMES 1:17

Forever

Born thy people to deliver,
Born a child, and yet a king,
Born to reign in us forever,
Now thy gracious kingdom bring.

CHARLES WESLEY

Rejoice,

that the immortal God is born,

so that mortal man may live in eternity.

JOHN HUSS

Christ's words are permanent

value because of His person;

they endure because He endures.

W. H. GRIFFITH THOMAS

In my Father's house are many rooms;

if it were not so,

I would have told you.

I am going there to prepare a place for you.

And if I go and prepare a place for you,

I will come back and take you to be with me

that you also may be where I am.

JOHN 14:2–3

❖   ❖   ❖

One day we will meet beside the river and

our Lord will dry every tear.

For now, we must live in the joy of that promise

and recall that for every generation life is hard,

but God is faithful.

BODIE THOENE

Faith is not knowing what the future holds,
but knowing who holds the future.

AUTHOR UNKNOWN

◆　　◆　　◆

*Now faith is being sure of what we hope
for and certain of what we do not see.*

HEBREWS 11:1

◆　　◆　　◆

And surely I am with you always,
to the very end of the age.

MATTHEW 28:20

I rejoice in the hope of that glory to be revealed,
for it is no uncertain glory that we look for. Our hope
is not hung upon such an untwisted thread as,
"I imagine so," or "It is likely," but the cable, the
strong tow of our fastened anchor, is the oath and
promise of Him who is eternal verity. Our salvation
is fastened with God's own hand, and with Christ's
own strength, to the strong stake of God's
unchangeable nature.

SAMUEL RUTHERFORD

*Jesus Christ is the same yesterday
and today and forever.*

◆　　◆　　◆

"Behold, I am coming soon!
My reward is with me,
and I will give to everyone according
to what he has done.
I am the Alpha and the Omega,
the First and the Last,
the Beginning and the End."

Give thanks to the Lord, for he is good;
his love endures forever.

PSALM 118:1

◆　　◆　　◆

'Twas love divine that Holy night
That came to make this dark world light.
He came to us from Heav'n above
To teach us how to live with love.
I'll serve Him till the end of time.
I'll tell the world of love divine;
True peace is mine—let come what may;
O! I'm so happy for Christmas Day.

WANDA ROYER

Are you willing to believe that love is the strongest thing in the world—stronger than hate, stronger than evil, stronger than death—and that the blessed life which began in Bethlehem nineteen hundred years ago is the image and brightness of the Eternal Love? Then you can keep Christmas.

HENRY VAN DYKE

ISBN 1-59310-407-3

Scripture quotations are taken from the HOLY BIBLE, NEW INTERNATIONAL VERSION®. NIV®. Copyright © 1973, 1978, 1984 by International Bible Society. Used by permission of Zondervan Publishing House. All rights reserved.

Poems by Wanda Royer are copyrighted and used by permission.

Cover image © Photonica

Published by Barbour Publishing, Inc., P.O. Box 719, Uhrichsville, Ohio 44683, www.barbourbooks.com

Our mission is to publish and distribute inspirational products offering exceptional value and biblical encouragement to the masses.

Member of the
Evangelical Christian
Publishers Association

Printed in China.
5 4 3 2 1